THE I AM FACTOR

THE I AM FACTOR

Copyright © 2019 Courtney Richards

Published by Beyond Expectations Media

ISBN 978-1-912845-17-0 (sc)

ISBN 978-1-912845-15-6 (e)

All rights reserved. No part of this publication may be reproduced, stored in a retrieval system, or be transmitted, in any form, or by any means, mechanical, electronic, photocopying or otherwise without prior written consent of the publisher.

Any people depicted in stock imagery provided by iStockphoto and Unsplash, are models and such images are being used for illustrative purposes only.

All Scripture quotations marked (NKJV) are from the New King James Version of the Bible. Copyright © 1979, 1980, 1982 by Thomas Nelson, Inc. Used by permission. All rights reserved.

All Scripture quotations marked (AMP) are from the Amplified Bible. Old Testament copyright © 1965, 1987 by Zondervan Corporation. The Amplified New Testament copyright © 1954, 1958, 1987 by the Lockman Foundation. Used by permission. All rights reserved.

All Scripture quotations marked (ESV) are from The Holy Bible, English Standard Version. Copyright © 2001 by Crossways Bibles. Used by permission. All rights reserved.

All Scripture quotations marked (NLT) are from the Holy Bible, New Living Translation. Copyright © 1996, 2004. Used by permission of Tyndale House Publishers. All rights reserved.

All Scripture quotations marked (EXB) are from The Expanded Bible, Copyright © 2011 Thomas Nelson Inc. All rights reserved.

Welcome!

Thank you for taking this journey today. I pray your investment of time is richly rewarded as you open your mind to wisdom and revelation truth about your relationships.

This program can eliminate years pain, disappointment and wasted experiences.

Life is always teaching us something. The lessons we learn from the situations of life are entirely based on our individual worldview. Do you live in a friendly or hostile universe? Einstein said the answer to this question is the most important decision you'll ever make.

3 Great Laws

- The Law of Entropy
- The Law of Observation
- The Law of the Seed

These 3 laws when combined together create something quite spectacular.

The Law of Entropy creates the understanding that we've been given delegated dominion & authority (Genesis 1:28) and unless we do something positive, nature (default position of chaos & disorder) will take its course. We have to enforce order. According to Psalm 1:1 (AMP), we are blessed when we choose not to be a passive and inactive bystander in the situations of life.

The way in which we see & perceive things (The Law of Observation) determines our emotions, our expectations and what we ultimately do about situations and circumstances around us; and The Law of the Seed teaches us that we have the ability and power to change our future by what we do with the seed in our possession today. We have the ability to root out bad seeds and plant new ones for a desired harvest.

Understanding and making use of this knowledge with fundamentally transform your relationships.

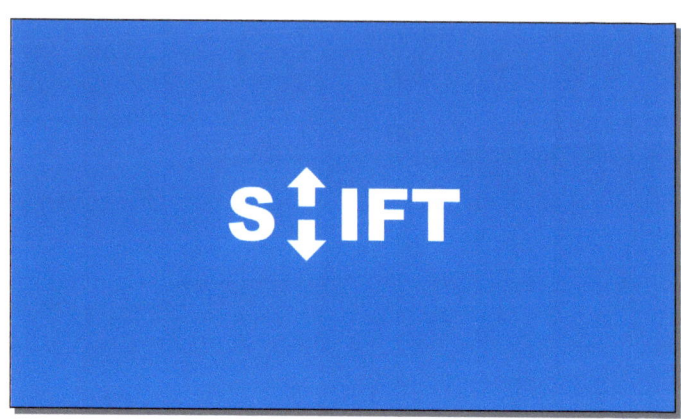

Ready, Steady, **SHIFT**

Please circle the Y = yes or the N = no, in answer to the following questions.

Ready

There is time in my life to invest in my own development	Y or N
A gap exists between where I want to be and where I am right now	Y or N
I can work on tasks that will help me to develop and grow	Y or N

Willing

I am willing to perform whatever is necessary to reach my goal and aims	Y or N
I am willing to SHIFT in my thinking concerning relationships and marriage	Y or N
I am willing to attempt new ways of achieving my goals	Y or N

Able

I have the commitment I need to succeed	Y or N
I have the support I need to make significant changes to my life	Y or N
I am mentally ready for a different approach to my life	Y or N
I am physically prepared for the encounters I may not have experienced before	Y or N

7-10 Y   This program will be effective, exciting and rewarding for you

5-7 Y   You may need to make some adjustments before starting this program

1-5 Y   You are not interested in SHIFTING!

What do you want to get from this program?

THE I AM FACTOR

Use the notes sections in this workbook to make notes whilst the facilitator takes you through the session.

> **Did you know** that there are around 250,000 marriages in Britain each year costing around £2.5Bn
>
> No-one gets married expecting to get divorced (unless it's a business arrangement). However, at a ratio of nearly 1 in 2 and costing around £40,000 per couple, there are around 115,000 divorces every year.

OUR AIM

Relating—and the quality of our relationships—is of deep, natural, and inherent concern for all of us and like any human endeavour, takes attention, care, and commitment. This program is designed to help you create a SHIFT in your thinking that supports the building of strong relationships allowing you to flourish whether single or married.

For those that are already married, it could serve as a means of identifying where things may have gone wrong and a platform for making things better.

You'll discover a possibility of being related independent of your past, your expectations, your preferences, or your views—a dimension more powerful than personality or circumstance—a dimension where relationships can become an occasion for creativity, vitality, intimacy, and self-expression.

Marriage Beyond Expectations:

- We offer specialist programs covering various aspects of improving relationships.
- We also offer Mediation/ Conflict Resolution service & Relationship Coaching
- Get in touch on 07957125137 or
  hello@marriagebeyondexpectations.com
  www.marriagebeyondexpectations.com

Do not be conformed to this world, but be transformed by the renewal of your mind, that by testing you may discern what is the will of God, what is good and acceptable and perfect. Romans 12:2 ESV

Our quest is to wage war on diseased thinking and to embed the divine truth.

CONTENTS

- Understand and break free from the mindset that gives rise to the abuse of self and others
- Understand the hidden mechanisms of abuse
- Strategies to break free into a place of liberation
- Strategies that promote a healthy self-image
- How to develop inner strength
- Inspire hope that drives action

Did you know?
26% of women and 15% of men aged 16 to 69 have experienced domestic abuse - 1:4 women and 1:6 men.

Do you have trouble speaking up or expressing yourself?

Have you ever seriously compromised your values or ideals to please others for the sake of it being easy or convenient?

I don't know about you, but **I HATE BULLIES!** Not a person per se, but more the act.
Not expressing my true feelings and compromising my values are two behaviours that have been very costly in large portions of my life. The real problem is that I didn't even recognise that it was happening.
To embark on a journey of change, I had to sit myself down and ask and answer the questions above.

Bullying is the ability to get someone to do something or act in a way they would otherwise have not done - like the playground bully that makes fear their weapon of choice in getting an individual to hand over their lunch or other possessions.

So, who or what's really influencing your actions?

From political parties and lobby groups to multi-national corporations and religious groups; influence is serious business. For those with less grand ambitions, like the playground bully, it is nonetheless important as every human relationship has some level of influence.

You see bullying, abuse and manipulation are types of influencing strategies, and they aren't as clear-cut and easy to spot as you might at first think...

Life revolves around people and with over 7.5 Billion of us on this rock called Earth - influencing is all about getting stuff done with and through others. This is achieved by positive and negative strategies - the key being identifying which road a relationship is going down.

And let them rule... Genesis 1:26
God created us (humans) and delegated authority for us to rule the planet and everything therein in accordance to His blueprint. Problems occur in all relationships when we try to rule in ways not according to the manufacturers' specifications.
According to the Crime Survey of England & Wales 2017, 26% of women and 15% of men report experiencing some form of domestic abuse. This doesn't include all the other types of relationships...

"A moment on the lips, a lifetime on the hips..." What influences us to follow pursuits we know are bad for us?
Consider those whose quest for the momentary gratification of a personal desire, influences them to make decisions that have regrettably had long term negative consequences.

Be it in a marriage or other significant relationship e.g. work, church, family members etc., many individuals feel trapped in an ever-decreasing circle of confinement and control not knowing that they can be free or how to go about it.

The intention of this program is to broaden your appreciation of what abuse really is in the context of your connections and to create a SHIFT in your thinking that supports the building of relationships that are fruitful and fit for purpose.

Self-Reflection

Are you having trouble speaking up or expressing yourself? **YES or NO**

Are you seriously compromising your values or ideals to please others for the sake of it being easy or convenient? **YES or NO**

Answering YES to either or both questions is a tell-tale sign of an abuse of self or others.

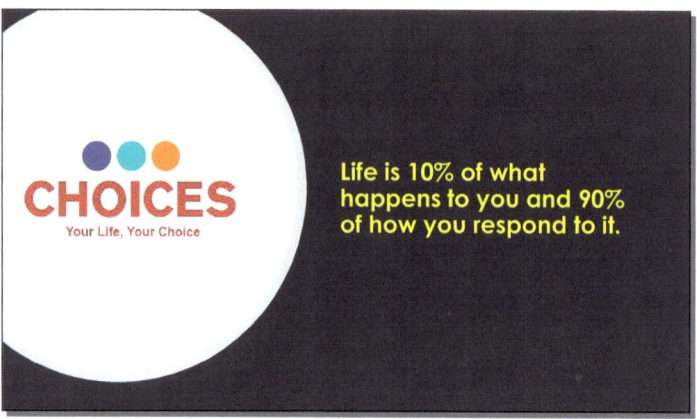

I call heaven and earth as witnesses today against you, that I have set before you life and death, blessing and cursing; therefore choose life, that both you and your descendants may live Deuteronomy 30:19 NKJV

We make choices every day, some simple, some not so. However, every choice that we make has a consequence. The life you live right now is based solely on the choices you've made (or others have made for you) in the past.

If we really think about it – there's a lot we can complain about, isn't there?

- Born the wrong sex
- Born the wrong colour
- Wrong height
- Our family
- Our life
- Our health
- Our Jobs
- Been abused
- Financial situation etc

The fact is – life is less about what's happened to you and more about what you do about it – the choices you make.

We are responsible for our choices (not our parents, spouses, friends or religious leaders).
There is one thing that God gave to every human being and it's the power of choice. The passage above states that He makes us responsible and calls the totality of the universe (heaven and earth) to be a witness to our choices.
Every choice leads to a consequence – intended or unintended.

Doing nothing is also a choice

You cannot keep birds from flying over your head, but you can keep them from building a nest in your hair. This Martin Luther quote has at its heart choice.

What are your choices costing you?

Failure or success – neither just happens.

IN THE KNOWLEDGE THAT EVERY CHOICE LEADS TO A CONSEQUENCE, **WHAT WILL YOU CHOOSE?**

The law of unintended consequences

Fuelled by the mindset of *"oh for a quiet life"* I compromised my values trying to make the marriage work. The unintended consequence being that my marriage failed – not exercising personal control and withdrawing from conflict being big factors.

The unintended consequence of not taking control of your life is that by default we are often handing control to someone or something else.

Action stations

- Am I being proactive or reactive?
- Did I make good choices today?
- Did I blame someone else today?

In what ways can replace complaining about your situation and instead start taking control of your life so that the choices you make are intentional ones?

Without understanding the purpose of a thing... abuse is inevitable.

On 15 Oct 2017, actress Alyssa Milano posted on Twitter: "If you've been sexually harassed or assaulted write 'me too' as a reply to this tweet." Twenty-four hours after her tweet, Milano had 500,000 replies.

While this related primarily to sexual harassment or abuse against women, the fact is that many people in all walks of life have been on the receiving end of some form of abusive behaviour where one person takes advantage over another with the misuse of power.

Uncovering the underlying cause

Be it using a device like a new smart phone, a machine like a car or a human life: To understand the highest/ correct use of a thing or human being we must by necessity consult the manufacturers mind (handbook) to understand their intention.

Abuse is simply the result of an incorrect or inappropriate use of a thing not in accordance with the manufacturer's original intent.

Therefore, without understanding the intended purpose of a thing abuse will always be inevitable...

This is especially true when it comes to human relationships.

From close friends to intimate relationships, from political parties to corporations advertising their products, from family members to team members in a work function; these interactions become abusive when we fail to understand how to influence correctly and we end up taking a route of getting what we want at the detriment of another.

There is also self-abuse including eating disorders like bulimia at one end and gluttony at the other.

Values. What are they and what do they have to do with influence and abuse? They:

- are an integral part of who we think we are
- are our moral principles and beliefs about what is valuable and important in life
- guide us in the decisions and choices we make
- demonstrated in how we behave

Values lie at the heart of our behaviours much the same as the relationship between a seed and the fruit that the tree bares. Just as a seed can only produce a pre-determined fruit, our values will always produce a pre-determined set of behaviours.

Being shaped by our upbringing, education, culture, life experiences etc, we all have different values, beliefs and opinions that shapes the way we live our lives, so your opinions won't necessarily match up with whom you share significant relationships with (at home, work or church).

What happens when values are in conflict?
Because values are so much about 'who we think we are' we'll often feel uneasy when they're in conflict with others. As a result, we can attempt to persuade another person to act in accordance with our values (consciously or unconsciously).
It's important to recognise that influence can be positive or negative as well as intentional or unintentional.

In relationships it could be used as a tool for selfishly getting one's own way or as a means to inspire positive change that really helps the other.

When we start working at a new company, we are often told about the corporate values and behaviours and are asked to adopt them while in the employment of that organisation. This is done to ensure consistency and a shared focus for all employees to shape the culture of the business.

ACTION STEP

Our heavenly father has a set of values and behaviours that He has given to us to benchmark against our current values and behaviours. Make the necessary changes to adopt the Kingdom culture.

What has God said about you?

3 GREAT LAWS

- **Law of Seed**
- **Law of Entropy**
- **Law of Observation**

Everything on earth follows certain laws, and it is important to recognise that the default position of everything in creation is chaos. The term "without form" found in Genesis 1:2 is the Hebrew word – Tohuw, and its meaning includes confusion and a place of chaos. Therefore, resolving chaos was the first thing God did in creation.

Seed. Everything reproduces after its own kind with exponential multiplication – even a thought. Being given seed means you have dominion and power of choice as to the seeds we sow or the one's we allow to be sown in the soil of our mind **AND THAT INCLUDES YOU**.

Entropy. Everything left to its own devices; without maintenance or some other form of intervention will inevitable break down, fall into disrepair, ruin or loss of energy/ power **AND THAT INCLUDES YOU**.

Observation. Things and situations in our lives will conform to the way we see them **AND THAT INCLUDES YOU**.

En route to possessing your divine purpose you'll encounter the gravitational pressure of circumstances and people issues.
Pressure is a fact of life so you might as well just accept it instead of praying and hoping for a pressure-less life – in fact, the only time that happens is when you're dead.

DECLARATION OF INTENT

Today, I choose to take responsibility for the results in my life.

Are you SHIFTING?

For example, I thought……. (old beliefs, I now reject), today I'm moving towards (new beliefs)……

I AM what I look like
I AM what I have (possessions)
I AM what I do (job/ career)
I AM what others think of me
I AM what my past says of me
I AM separate from God

Your ego is nothing more than an idea that you have about yourself.

As you cannot rise above your confession, what are you saying about yourself? And who are you becoming?

- Does it line up with the picture of the future you really want to create?

- Knowing that stagnation is a form of decline, are you thriving or just surviving?

The I AM statements above are all ego standpoints (identity statements) that will take your life in a direction away from what God created you to be.

The first temptation mentioned in the Bible related to identity (Genesis 3), *has God really said...?* Questioning and taking a different opinion to your creator. As a result, the first Adam fell and consigned mankind to slavery. However, to redeem mankind the last Adam (Jesus) had to overcome the same identity issue when challenged by the devil when he asked, *"if you are the son of God, command these stone to be made bread"*.

So, are you performing to prove your identity or performing from your identity?

Be clear on the fact that your identity comes from who your father is... Knowing your identity comes from a relationship with your father.

Like the many superheroes depicted in films, we often wear masks to hide our true identity because it helps other people feel comfortable around us.
Don't settle for second best - **Choose** to be all that God called you to be.

Your true identity is not defined by your looks, possessions, job, what others think of you or your past – they are all masks!

Define the picture of yourself that's deep in your heart?
Move towards that goal with passion.

You are a spirit created in God's image and likeness, with a soul (housing your mind) and a body.

This is relevant because, you are therefore not your mind.
This means you can change it if you wish... your thinking and attitudes are all up for change...

We've all had different experiences of life and family ranging from that which was being supportive to traumatic and everything in between... However, the tragedy with failure is not knowing what caused the failure. The tragedy with success is not knowing what caused the success.
This way you won't know what to repeat, or what to stop doing. **Therefore, in all your getting, get understanding.**

There is something that is visible in the lives of all uncommon achievers - no matter their experiences or start in life, they knew that they could work towards a great end that they could pass onto their children, and others around them.

> **EXERCISE**
> List some ways in which you've changed your mind over the last 12 months – even if they are little things. Go further back if necessary.
>
>
> You see, you're already an expert at SHIFTING YOUR THINKING!
>
> *When I was a child, I spoke as a child, I understood as a child, I thought as a child; but when I became a man, I put away childish things.*

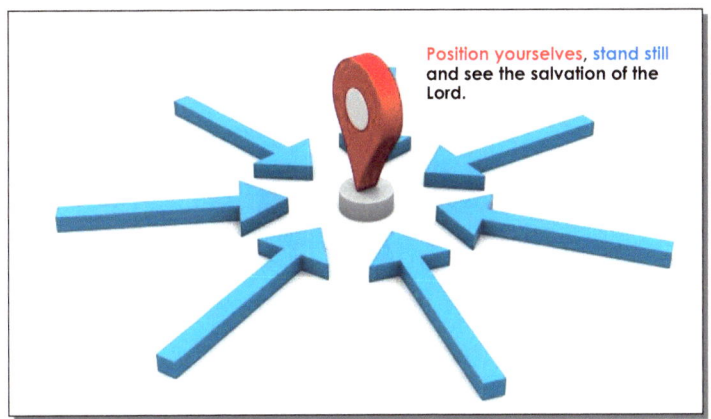

G od created everything with a purpose and intent, and commanded every living thing to produce more – **that includes you.**

In His system of interdependency my produce feeds another person's need and ability to produce themselves. For example, a carrot grows and supplies the need for growth in a rabbit and birds spreading flower pollens. Everything has its necessary function and place in creation – **that includes you.**

My failure to produce will therefore affect not just me, but those that are reliant on what I would have produced - this is why God calls failure to produce wicked – (Matt 25:26).

Welfare, prosperity, deliverance, preservation, salvation, safety, healing, preserve, do well, be made whole. All the preceding words encompass the word *salvation*.

The image shown above is a location icon symbolising positioning oneself.

In this example taken from 2 Chronicles 20:17, the condition for experiencing the salvation package is that you place your focus on God, get into the position the He created for you and remain there (stand still).

1. **Focus on God** – In Him we live and move and have our being (Acts 17:28) – by placing our focus on Him we overcome distractions and other influential forces.
2. **Finding your position** – Finding your position involves knowing what God has created you and only you to do and pursuing that high calling in the knowledge that it's is your reasonable service to your King.
3. **Stay there** – Standing still takes work! This is about maintaining a resolute focus on doing what God has told you in the knowledge that

you and only you will have to give account for your fulfilment of what He's commanded you.

Some of us have got into problems by being out of position. Others have the tenacity and staying power – the only problem being they're in the wrong position. Both standpoints will not see the full salvation that the Lord promised.

You may believe you have nothing to offer, but the truth is that the **totality of creation needs you to be the real you**. Don't allow any form of inducement or people pressure to move you from your place by accepting a version of yourself that God did not create.

In my opinion, one of the saddest stories in the Bible relates to the consequences of being moved out of position - Young vs. Old prophet 1 Kings 13:11-25 – against the backdrop of a culture where respecting your elders was a core value enshrined in their society, the young prophet was moved by the manipulative influential pressure of a senior prophet with a covert agenda. As a consequence, he put pleasing man above obeying God and was tragically killed.

Being moved out of you position will cost not just you but everyone around you that's dependent on the produce of your fruit.

> **Action step**
>
> Ask God to give you wisdom and revelation to understand what He has called you to be.

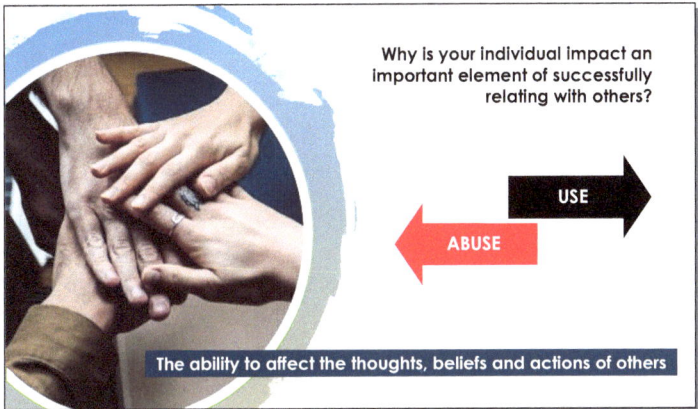

Without question the most prized quality with leaders past and present is their ability (power) to influence others to action, and as we glance through history, we see leaders using this quality with powerful effectiveness from evil to good.

This applies not just to leaders, but co-workers. Not just co-workers but in marriage. Not just in marriage but in relationships with friends and family.

The use of negative influence tactics like avoiding, manipulating, intimidating, and threatening have their origin in a fear and shortage mindset – based on a focus on survival not growth. Whereas rational persuasion, inspirational appeals, consultation and collaboration are examples of positive influence based on a growth mindset.

The ability to influence another person is a power that can be used or abused. If God wants to bless you He will often put a person in your life, the same is true for the devil when he plans to derail you.

> **Self-reflection**
> Regarding your significant relationships at home, work or church etc., whose side are you on when it comes to influence?
>
> Are you using or abusing your influence?

What is Power?

What circumstances give a person power?

Think about personal experience of feeling powerful or when you've felt powerless or vulnerable in a personal or work situation. What was it that made you feel powerful?

What did the other person have that made you feel vulnerable?

> I felt powerful/ powerless when...

Think of people who you think are powerful... e.g. lawyer, pastor, police, a celebrity, the queen, a nightclub bouncer. What is it that makes them powerful?

Power is the ability to produce an effect or to influence or direct events.

ower (or the perception of) can exist through:

1. **Position or connections** e.g. politician, police, religious leader, manager at work, a teacher, a celebrity etc. where authority has been conferred on an individual.
2. **Knowledge or expertise** e.g. encourages respect and influence
3. **Access to information** e.g. if the information is valuable to others
4. **Reward** e.g. the ability to reward through compliance
5. **Fear** e.g. punishment, harm, humiliation, disfavour - Do what I say or there'll be punishment. (Nebuchadnezzar's threat to the 3 Hebrew captives – bow or die! Likewise, the threat to Daniel in the time of Darius).
6. **Personality** e.g. potential to be influential by likeable/ admirable people or having an explosive personality that others egg-shell around or are wary of.

We all have different ways of being powerful – be aware of it and how and where we use it. Other circumstances giving power include:

The law gives power/ rights	Uniforms – associated with authority
Hierarchy / jobs	Charisma / charm
Sexual attraction/attractiveness	Peer group/can use peer pressure

RECOGNISE THAT YOU HAVE MORE POWER THAN YOU THINK

Abusive behaviour can take many forms. All forms of abusive behaviour are ways in which one human being is trying to control or have power over another.

These behaviours can include but are not limited to:
- Emotional / Psychological
- Isolation
- Intimidation
- Economic
- Physical
- Sexual

God gave man the fundamental right to choose. All forms of manipulation seeks to compromise your ability to make decisions that are balanced.

And God blessed them. And God said to them, "Be fruitful and multiply and fill the earth and subdue it, and have dominion over the fish of the sea and over the birds of the heavens and over every living thing that moves on the earth." Genesis 1:28

Following the above passage, here are three important questions about creation and mankind that need to be answered:

1. What was the purpose that God created man to fulfil?
God created man for rulership (dominion) and relationship, NOT RELIGION.

2. Who or what were we created to have dominion over?
God gave mankind dominion/ rulership & mastery over the fish, birds, livestock, over all the earth and over every creeping thing that creeps on the earth.

3. Who or what were not included in the answer to question 2?
Other humans. We were never given permission to dominate other humans - to do so is a violation of divine protocol and is tantamount to witchcraft.

Let's just clarify a part of the above passage… *over every living thing that moves on the earth* - the Hebrew word *ramas* relates to motion of smaller animals that creep on the ground, both those that have four or more legs – so this includes monkeys but certainly not humans!

We were created for relationships; with God and each other and every relationship has an element of influence

> *If submission is forced, it becomes ungodly control*

It wasn't long before mankind realised that you can get more done as a team that working alone... and in our inter-relatedness, the intention is to have a positive influence on each other based on a growth mindset of abundance, hope and love. This is achieved through employing tactics such as socialising, appealing, logical persuasion, consulting, alliance building etc.

Because God gave the earth to mankind with delegated authority, everything that happens on this planet occurs through a human being. This rings true even to the point that when mankind fell through Adam, he had to send his Son in the form of a man to redeem us and influence change.

If God wants to change the direction of your life, he directs a person to come into your life. The same principle works if the devil wants to destroy your destiny.

Some tactics to be aware of

- **Death by a thousand cuts** – here the method of control is by the use of frequent and continual badgering for example, Samson and Delilah – she wore him down with her words (judges 16:16)
- **Appealing to your pride** - wanting to be seen as a good Christian, good citizen, good parent etc.
- **Giving of gifts to create an obligation** – giving a gift with the motive of altering the recipient's objectivity in decision making e.g. accepting a bribe.
- **Narrowing your options or challenging you to make a choice based on your fear of shortage** – for example telling someone that the opportunity is time-limited – *you've got to act now…*
- **Gaslighting** – a term that refers to trying to convince someone they're wrong about something even when they aren't - making the other person question their sanity.
- **Ignoring** – creating isolation or using the silent treatment to generate action
- **Intimidation** - using physical violence or other threatening behaviour to generate action.
- **Sexual abuse** – using sex or sexual attraction to generate action.
- **Playing on their fears or boosting their ego** – repeatedly talking about negative or fear generating situations or the use of flattery.
- **Guilt tripping** – the strategic use of guilt in relationships to generate action towards or away from a thing.

WHO AM I?

- I am your constant companion.
- I am your greatest helper or heaviest burden.
- I will push you onward or drag you down to failure.
- I am completely at your command.
- Half of the things you do you might as well turn over to me and I will do them - quickly and correctly.
- I am easily managed - you must be firm with me.
- Show me exactly how you want something done and after a few lessons, I will do it automatically.
- I am the servant of great people, and alas, of all failures as well.
- Those who are great, I have made great.

WHO AM I?

- Those who are failures, I have made failures.
- I am not a machine though I work with the precision of a machine plus the intelligence of a person.
- You may run me for profit or run me for ruin - it makes no difference to me.
- Take me, train me, be firm with me, and I will place the world at your feet.
- Be easy with me and I will destroy you.
- **Who am I?**

* Answer on next page

> **TODAY I CHOOSE TO EXCHANGE ONE BAD HABIT FOR A BETTER ONE**

I AM HABIT

Habits are things we do repeatedly.
Most of the time we are hardly aware that we have them as they're on autopilot.

Some habits are bad...
- Blame all of your problems on your parents, your spouse, your religious leaders, your crappy neighbourhood, the government, or something or somebody else.
- Always put off your taking action until tomorrow.
- Staying away from good books, nature, or anything else that may inspire you
- Live for the moment & never plan ahead

Some habits are good...
- Exercising regularly and eating sensibly
- Planning ahead
- Showing respect for others
- Taking responsibility for your actions

Some just don't matter...
- Reading magazines from back to front
- Eating pizza with your hands

When thinking about habits, ask yourself is it taking me in the direction I want to go?

FIRST, WE MAKE OUR HABITS, THEN OUR HABITS MAKE US

WHY ME?
Being honest with yourself

In response to experiencing abusive control, a common and natural response by many is to ask, *why me?*

At the heart of all abusive behaviours is the presence of selfishness. This also happens to be the opposite of love.

Do you view life through a mirror or a window?

Seeing life through the perspective of a mirror will mean that all your decisions are driven by selfish motives. Seeing life through the perspective of a window means that your decisions are driven by the motive of love causing you to be outward looking to God and people.

The danger of using the mirror is that all you ever see is yourself causing heightened anxiety and the need to look after oneself at all costs.

…every person is tempted when he is drawn away, enticed and baited by his own evil desire (lust, passions). James 1:14 AMP

The shocking truth is that in many (but not all) cases both the person experiencing, and the perpetrator of the abuse share a common goal – in that they are modifying their behaviour to get a favourable outcome for themselves from someone else. Put another way in the image above the fish is searching for food and spots something that looks like it and starts to pursue it. The fisherman with bait is also searching – searching for a fish that's hungry and not paying attention.

For example, my passionate desire to be accepted caused me to tolerate behaviours in a relationship - behaviours that were in violation of my own personal values because receiving acceptance was more important to me at that time.

I could complain that I was the recipient of abuse, and yes in some ways that is true. However, I too was modifying my behaviour in the game of abuse by not upholding my values and risking the rejection.

> As a rabbit is lured out of his burrow, so man by lust is allured from the safety of self-restraint to sin.
>
> To entice a victim into a moral trap, luring them in through their own selfish impulses.

Self-reflection

Your own lust - what's in it for me?

1. Identify what you are getting out of the deal?
2. What are you really hoping to achieve?
3. Start to become aware of your internal motivations.

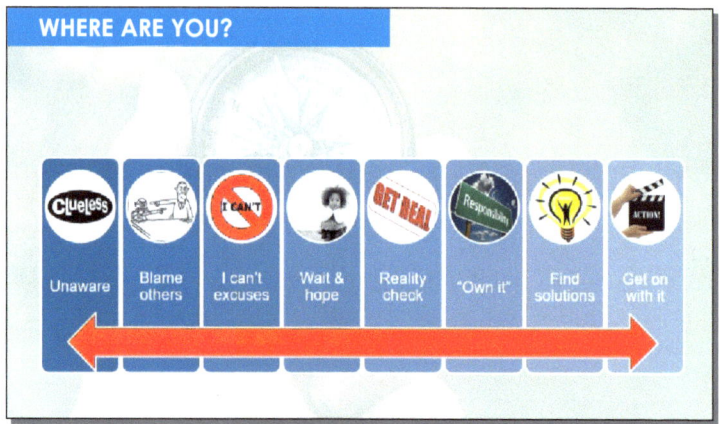

When faced with issues of life, it is important to recognise that you are only in charge of your own behaviour – you are not in control of what another person does. Therefore, you are either part of the problem or part of the solution. You choose how you want to react...

When faced with challenges, do you feel powerful or powerless?

> ... *He who is in you is greater than he who is in the world.* 1 John 4:4

Instead of seeing yourself defined by the situation e.g. I AM a victim, or I AM an abuser – recognise that these are identity statements that will determine your future. See yourself as a creation of the Most High God who has experienced or perpetrated abuse (mistreatment), but can make decisions to change your story...

But I AM angry, hurt, damaged etc. and want to stay that way

While it's normal to be angry, if your finding that years later you're still feeling the intensity of the situation or are still stuck – know that the vexation you feel is rooted not in what the other person did in the past, but in how you're reacting to it right now.

- In the knowledge that if you're learning you're not losing, what can you learn from the situation?
- What is it in you that's causing you to be stuck?

Seeing it as an event and not an identity-defining moment will help you reframe it, take control of your life and move on with your divine purpose and stop allowing yourself to be defined by events of the past.

Are you SHIFTING?

For example, I thought……. (old beliefs, I now reject), today I'm moving towards (new beliefs)……

Nip things in the bud!
Conduct allowed is conduct approved

Is fear preventing you from communicating effectively?

Start to recognise that conduct allowed is conduct approved in that failure to speak up by default is giving consent – tacit approval.

1. Recognise the importance of knowing your values and what's acceptable to you.
2. In your relationships, it's far easier to nip things in the bud by dealing with them with them when they first arise than trying to overhaul a habit that's taken root over many years of avoidance.
3. Recognise that avoidance just makes things worse in the long run.
4. Get use to giving feedback as it helps others know where they stand with you and it's a form of honesty.
5. Don't feel like you have to begrudgingly nod in agreement to everything in an attempt to keep the peace. Say what you think respectfully, but don't deny yourself your right to expression. Value your opinions and others will, too.
6. Overcome the disease to please – by knowing how to say NO when things don't work for you or fit into your schedule etc.
7. Stop trying to make others happy – joy come from being in God's presence not yours.
8. Remember that *God is able to keep you from falling* – Jude 1:25, and that *nothing can separate me from his love*... Romans 8:38-39

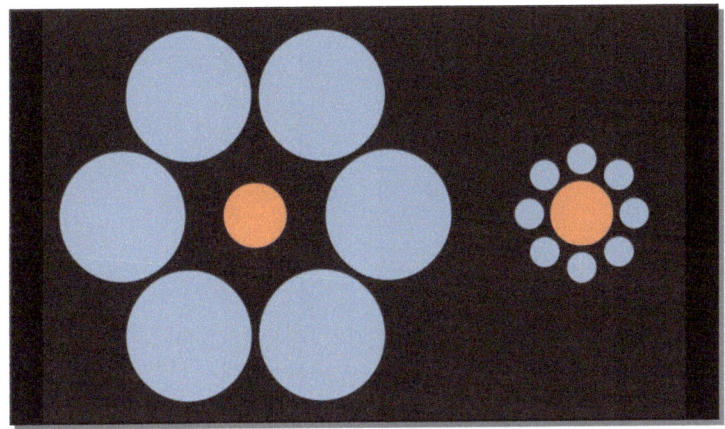

Look at the two orange dot's in the pictures. Which is larger?

Would you believe me if I told you they were exactly the same size?

What does that teach us about life?

...these other men who tell you how important they are! But they are only comparing themselves with each other, using themselves as the standard of measurement. How ignorant! 2 Corinthians 10:12b NLT

In a world of comparisons, we often find that we don't measure up. In fact, you'll never measure up to someone else's model of the world.
Comparing your life with another will also weaken your position – causing you to **lose perspective** and **become open to abusive control**.

A trick of many con artists is the art of distraction – by getting you to focus on something else (away from the necessary details), you become more liable to fall for their scheme. The more you compare your life, your gifts and your calling to others the less likely you'll succeed in fulfilling what has called you to do on the earth.

How should we look at the lives of others?
For inspiration, but not for competitive-based comparison

...keeping our eyes on Jesus, the champion who initiates and perfects our faith. Hebrews 12:2

BEING YOU

- You are an individual, and that's okay...

- It's better to be a 1st rate you, than a 2nd rate someone else!

- Comparison is the thief of joy

You have to be a human being before you can be a human doing!

There are similarities, but no copies in creation.

Recognise that our god is a God of diversity and that you are fearfully and wonderfully made – perfect just at you are.

That you are valuable and special and it's better to be a 1st rate you than a 2nd rate someone else (you'll only truly be happy when you're in the place God created for you).

Are you SHIFTING?

For example, I thought……. (old beliefs, I now reject), today I'm moving towards (new beliefs)……

In today's modern world we can buy in assistance for almost every area of our lives. However, managing your personal boundaries is a job only you can do. Failure to manage your boundaries will always result in some form of abuse.

Aggressive behaviour does not respect the personal boundaries of others and thus are liable to harm others while trying to influence them. Characterised by:
- Hostility
- Putting down other people
- Not allowing people to choose for themselves

Some examples of aggressive language
- You're mad!
- Do it my way!
- You make me sick!
- Sarcasm, name calling, threatening, blaming insulting

At the heart of aggressiveness is the spirit of manipulation and ungodly control - witchcraft.

Passive behaviour doesn't defend their own personal boundaries and thus allow the aggressive to harm or otherwise unduly influence them. They are also typically not likely to risk trying to influence anyone else. Characterised by:
- Denial of own feelings/opinions
- Allowing others to choose for you
- Guilt, anger

Some examples of passive language
- Oh, it's nothing

- Oh, that's all right; I didn't want it anymore
- Why don't you go ahead and do it; my ideas aren't very good anyway

Assertiveness is a state of mind – knowing what your rights are and standing up for them without violating the rights of others!"

Given to making bold assertions, assertiveness is a trait that's linked to self-esteem and considered an important communication skill.
A person who communicates assertively is not afraid to speak his or her mind or trying to influence others but doing so in a way that respects the personal boundaries of others. They are also willing to defend themselves against aggressive behaviour. Characterised by:
- Open, direct self-expression of your thoughts and feelings
- Allowing others to choose for themselves
- Mutual satisfaction at achieving a desired goal

Assertive language
- I am…
- I think we should…
- I feel bad when…
- That seems unfair to me
- Can you help me with this?

Assertive language is rooted in the understanding of speaking the truth in love. Ephesians 4:15

How to spot if you're in an abusive situation (of self or others):

- Not able to speak for yourself
- The need to hide aspects of your life from others
- The need to lie or shade the truth

WINNERS MINDSET

Essential steps to being a winner

- Know that you are already a winner
- Start with the end in mind
- Mind your own business – be consumed with it, having zero tolerance for distractions, discouragement or comparisons with others.

1. Know that you are already a winner.
2. Start with the end in mind – based on what God has revealed to you.
3. Mind your own business – be consumed with it, having zero tolerance for distractions, discouragement or comparisons with others.
4. Winners are hungry and won't settle for less
5. Winners know they are here for a purpose
6. They fall down but they still have the strength to get back up and try again.
7. They know failure isn't final.
8. They overcome the anger of past events in the knowledge that their future is bigger and brighter than their past. They learn from it and move forward.
9. They know how to let go of the past and move past yesterday's story.
10. They refuse to give up.
11. They finish strong.

What questions do I have?

NOTES

Also available from Beyond Expectations Media

Thinking Fit For Marriage

Built to Last

Making Difference Work

Chaos to Order

Through the Storm

Untying Fear Knots

Eye to Eye

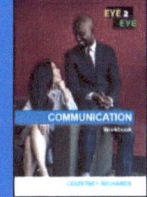

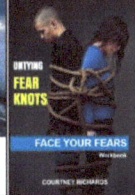

GYMNASIUM
OF THE MIND